SAFARI READERS

3

BOOK STAGE

Penguins

SAFARI
READERS

Tristan Walters

For Billy & Phoebe

– the original Safari Readers!

Copyright © 2019 Safari Readers

www.safarireaders.com

Written & Designed by Tristan Walters

Magellanic Penguin

Abbreviations - FreeVectorMaps (FVM); Shutterstock (SS). Cover (background), Nattle/SS; Cover (middle), Jan Martin Will/SS; 1, Sergey Uryadnikov/SS; 2 -3, Anton Ivanov/SS; 3, Zhenyakot/SS; 4, Earth Trotter Photos/SS; 5 (top left), Colacat/SS; 5 (top right), Coulangeo/SS; 5 (bottom left), Michaela Klenkova/SS; 5 (bottom middle), Galina Savina/SS; 5 (bottom right), Jiri Prochazka/SS; 6, ValerieVSNB/SS; 6-7 (background), MidoSemsem/SS; 6-7 (middle), Eric Isselee/SS; 8, Stephen Belcher/SS; 9, Amplion/SS; 10, Volodymyr Goinyk/SS; 11, FreeVectorMaps/FVM; 11, Photosky/SS; 12, HelloRZFcool/SS; 13, Pngimages/SS; 14-15, BMJ/SS; 16, Andre Anita/SS; 17, Earth Trotter Photos/SS; 18, Vadim Nefedoff/SS; 19, A7880S/SS; 20, Roger Clark ARPS/SS; 21 (adult), Ondrej Prosicky/SS; 21 (nest), TravelMediaProductions/SS; 21 (egg), Buenaventura/SS; 21 (chick), Roger Clark ARPS/SS; 22, Stu Shaw/SS; 23, getfile/SS; 25, Sararoom Design/SS; 26, Jo Crebbin/SS; 28, Sergey Novikov/SS; Back (background), Nattle/SS; Back (bottom right), macrovector/SS. Animation Images (back, 5, 7, 9, 11, 13, 19, 23-28), Memo Angeles/SS.

Contents

What is a penguin?

Chinstrap Penguin

Penguins are a kind of bird. Like all other birds, penguins have feathers and lay eggs. Unlike most other birds, penguins cannot fly.

FLIGHTLESS BIRDS

Can you name each of the flightless birds?

Emu
(Australia)

Ostrich
(Africa)

Kakapo
(New Zealand)

Cassowary
(Australia)

Kiwi
(New Zealand)

What does a penguin look like?

PENGUIN

SCIENTIFIC NAME
Sphenisciformes

SIZE
Up to 1.2m tall

WEIGHT
Up to 40 kg

SPEED
30 km per hour

AGE
Up to 20 years

short feathers

keeps the penguin warm

webbed feet

helps the penguin to steer

Penguins are **aquatic** birds. They have a sleek body for swimming and a thick layer of fat to keep them warm in the cold water.

Check out the words in **bold** in our glossary on the back page.

hooked bill

holds onto slippery fish

African Penguin

Can you read and match each label on the penguin?

strong flippers

powers the penguin to swim

What types of penguin are there?

ADELIE PENGUIN
7,000,000
POPULATION

Did you know?
Adelie penguins are one of the most common kinds of penguin.

There are eighteen kinds of penguin in the world. The emperor penguin is the tallest and the little blue penguin is the shortest.

TYPES OF PENGUIN

Yellow-eyed

Royal

Chinstrap

Gentoo

King

Emperor

Humboldt

Erect-crested

African

Magellanic

Which penguin do you like the most?

Macaroni

Adelie

Fiordland

Rockhopper

Snares

Galapagos

White-flippered

Little Blue

Where do penguins live?

Gentoo Penguin

Did you know?
The south pole, or **Antarctica**, is the coldest place on the planet.

-50°C

Many penguins live on the islands and coasts near the South Pole. Penguins are also found in warmer places, like Africa and Australia.

Which direction is south on the map?

Arctic Ocean

PARCHED PENGUIN

Penguins can live in temperatures as hot as 40°C!

Atlantic Ocean

Pacific Ocean

N

Pacific Ocean

Indian Ocean

S

= penguin habitat

Southern Ocean

SOUTH POLE
(ANTARCTICA)

How deep can penguins dive?

Did you know?
Emperor penguins can hold their breath for 22 minutes!

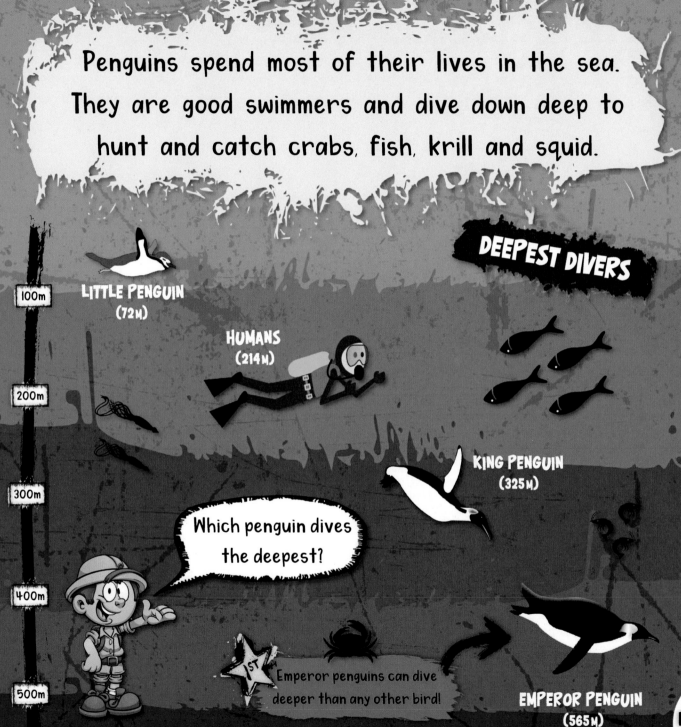

Penguins spend most of their lives in the sea. They are good swimmers and dive down deep to hunt and catch crabs, fish, krill and squid.

DEEPEST DIVERS

100m

LITTLE PENGUIN
(72M)

HUMANS
(214M)

200m

300m

KING PENGUIN
(325M)

Which penguin dives the deepest?

400m

1ST Emperor penguins can dive deeper than any other bird!

500m

EMPEROR PENGUIN
(565M)

13

Why do penguins march?

King Penguin

Did you know?
Some penguins march over 80km to get to their feeding site!

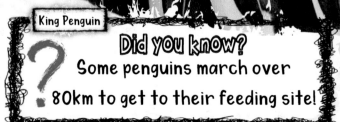

Some penguins have to travel a long way to get to their feeding sites. They are slower on land and have to waddle, jump or slide to move around.

How many penguins live in a colony?

Penguins live and nest together on land in a huge group, called a **colony**. Some colonies can have over one million penguin pairs.

Penguins will often huddle together to keep themselves warm in the ❄ cold winters. ❄

PENGUIN COLONY

Some penguin colonies are so big you can see them from space!

Penguins often nest in the same place every year.

Zavodovski Island (South Atlantic) has a colony of over two million chinstrap penguins!

What predators does a penguin have?

> **Did you know?**
> **?** Penguins make lots of noises and even have a call to scare **predators**

Lots of animals hunt penguins. In the sea, they face threats from sharks and **aquatic** mammals. On land, they are hunted by foxes and birds.

PENGUIN PREDATORS

LEOPARD SEAL

Penguins return to the ice quickly to avoid any hiding leopard seals.

SKUA

Penguins huddle together to keep chicks hidden from attacking skuas.

Can you name the penguin **predators**?

ORCA

Penguins zig zag in the water to escape from orcas.

How many chicks do penguins have?

All penguins live in pairs. They will stay with their mate all their lives and take it in turns to look after and feed their one, or two chicks.

PENGUIN LIFECYCLE

ADULT

Each penguin has its own call that it uses to find its mate.

NEST

Penguins like to nest in rocky or sheltered places.

After their first moult, chicks leave the nest to go fishing.

YOUNG

EGG

Emperor and King penguins lay one egg and other penguins lay two.

The chicks hatch after two months and are fed and kept warm by the parents.

CHICK

Why are penguins in trouble?

Did you know?
The **Antarctic** is warming five times faster than the rest of the world!

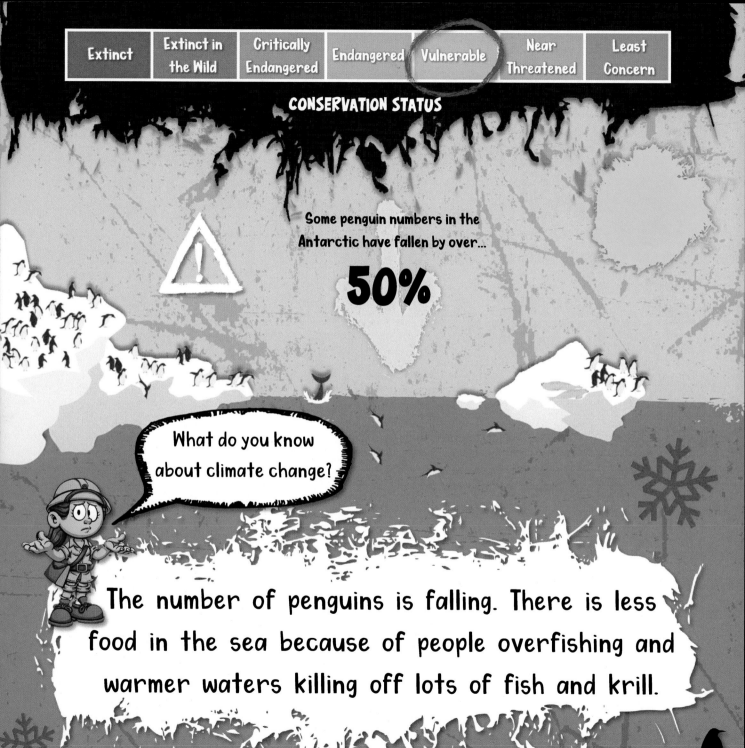

Extinct	Extinct in the Wild	Critically Endangered	Endangered	Vulnerable	Near Threatened	Least Concern

CONSERVATION STATUS

Some penguin numbers in the Antarctic have fallen by over...

50%

What do you know about climate change?

The number of penguins is falling. There is less food in the sea because of people overfishing and warmer waters killing off lots of fish and krill.

Penguin Puzzle

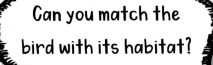

Can you match the bird with its habitat?

wetlands

Antarctic

rainforest

desert

24

Safari Readers

The 'Safari Readers' books are specially designed to help children learn to read. Based on leading teaching practice, this series enables children to develop a range of reading skills and create a love of reading and language through wild and exciting topics.

Enjoy the ride!

Reading is fun! These books are best enjoyed when reading together.

The child may need some help reading the smaller text.

The larger text is for the child to read.

There is a book for all our 'Safari Readers' out there.

Why not join 'Safari Sam' and 'Safari Suzy' and explore the other books we have in the series!

STAGE 1

Cheetahs · Flamingos · Wolves · Giraffes · Dolphins

STAGE 2

Sea Turtles · Tigers · Elephants · Polar Bears · Gorillas

Sharks · Lions · Penguins ✓ · Snakes · Monkeys

STAGE 3

For more information check out our website:

WWW.SAFARIREADERS.COM

Glossary

Can you remember all of the new words we have learnt?

Aquatic an animal or plant that spends most of its life on or in water.

Antarctica the coldest and most southern of the world's seven continents.

Habitat the area or place where an animal lives.

Colony a group of animals living together.

Predator an animal that hunts and feeds on another animal.

Made in the USA
Monee, IL
19 March 2021